PANORAMA OF AMERICAN HORSES

design by Len Jossel

PANORAMA OF AMERICAN HORSES

by Steven D. Price

A Media General Publication   Richmond, Virginia

Westover
Publishing Company

Prepared in cooperation with Photo Researchers, Inc.,
New York, New York.

CONTENTS

FOREWORD

The role of the horse in America has been made familiar to everyone since childhood. A baby is bounced on a parent's knee to the rhythm of "Ride A Cock Horse." Nursery and elementary school songs include "The Old Grey Mare," "Goodbye Old Paint," and "The Camptown Races." Young girls weep over the adventures of "Black Beauty" and "National Velvet" while their brothers brandish six-shooters in imitation of cowboy heroes. Teachers made us memorize "Paul Revere's Ride" and read about The Headless Horseman in "The Legend of Sleepy Hollow" while classroom posters and history books depicted George Washington astride his white charger. Social studies chronicled horse-and-buggy days, followed by the Iron Horse and horsepower. High school and college introduced us to, among others, MOBY DICK's White Stallion of the West (a far more agreeable creature than the whale and its pursuers), John Steinbeck's "The Red Pony," and that passage in "John Brown's Body" where Benet described the esteem in which Southerners held their mounts:

> The jewels of the horseman's hands and thighs,
> They go by the word and hardly need the rein.
> They bred such horses in Virginia then,
> Horses that were remembered after death
> And buried not so far from Christian ground.

Other equine influences continue to surround us. Scarcely a television hour goes by without some kind of "head 'em off at the pass" or "hold my horse, my good man" Western or historical movie, punctuated by advertisers associating their wares with the virility of the cowboy, social status of the foxhunting set, or speed and maneuverability of a range horse. The advent of off-track betting has increased radio and newspaper coverage of Thoroughbred and harness racing. And although the U.S. Army abolished its cavalry units more than twenty years ago, the sight of a riderless horse at state funerals remains an enduring symbol.

The horse, however, has not become an anachronism. There are at the present writing approximately eight million of them of which more than three-quarters are pleasure mounts. Operating a riding establishment is a profitable type of enterprise, particularly in conjunction with boarding, training, and equitation instruction, since increased leisure time has made horseback riding one of the country's fastest-growing activities. Its popularity is nationwide. New York

City's Central Park is the setting for the old-world elegance of an elderly couple, the woman riding sidesaddle, on a matched pair of greys smartly stepping along the bridle paths. Far away geographically but close in spirit is a family enjoying a dude ranch vacation, traveling across a mountain pasture on reliable horses to a chuck wagon barbecue and campfire. Teenagers wearing bathing suits cantering along a California beach differ from scarlet-clad North Carolina fox hunters only in formality, certainly not in enjoyment.

Enthusiasm for horses cuts across generations. A Midwestern boy learns from his grandfather how to train draft horses for county fair weight-pulling contests. Young girls have schoolroom daydreams about blue ribbons until it is time to race to local stables and favorite mounts. Most summer camps include the activity as one of the most popular, with campers getting up before sunrise to go on pre-breakfast rides. Apprentice jockeys listen to more experienced colleagues discuss racetrack strategy and lore in the hope that they too will ride the fastest of the world's fastest animals. Students at Western schools win varsity letters for competing in intercollegiate rodeos. Suburban housewives sandwich an hour's hacking between carpools and shopping trips, and when dinner talk turns to riding, they and their children persuade Daddy to try. He does, likes it in spite of stiff muscles, and joins several commuter pals in an evening's instruction class at the stable.

Although the histories of breeds in America begins with the horses brought by Spanish and British explorers, the colonial period was not the first time the North American continent contained that type of animals. Some sixty million years ago a small, four-toed quadruped named *eohippus* flourished on the grassy plains east of the Rocky Mountains. Its size increased and its middle toes merged into a hoof (the fetlock is a vestigial reminder of the other two) as *eohippus* evolved into *equus caballus*, the species we now know. Whether disease or geophysical disaster, something occurred approximately ten thousand years ago to drive these horses to extinction on this continent, but not before bands migrated across the Bering Strait and eastern Asia to Northern Europe and the Middle East. Those which gravitated to northern climates developed into taller, heavyset creatures to withstand the cold; others which reached deserts became smaller and lean. These are, respectively, the cold and warm

FOREWORD

breed types, the more direct ancestors of our modern breeds.

To delve into the origins of various breeds found, if not founded, in this country is to realize the interrelated backgrounds of so many of them, making them brothers under the hide. Thoroughbreds and pacers created Morgans and Standardbreds. The American Saddle Horse came from Thoroughbreds, Morgans, and pacers. Crosses with draft breeds created hunter-types, while Quarter horses are descended from wild mustangs, Morgans, and Thoroughbreds. America's reputation as a melting pot is nowhere more in evidence than in the heritage of its equine population.

There are certain words and phrases which you will encounter throughout this book with perhaps disconcerting frequency. "Bold," "willing," and "handy," for example—anthropomorphic expressions applied to certain members of all breeds meaning perhaps no more than these animals do what their owners or riders ask of them. But the respect and affection in which people hold horses have to be expressed some way, and how else to capture in language the extra effort a jumper makes to clear a six-foot obstacle, the way a Thoroughbred or Standardbred hangs on to reach the finish line ahead of all others, or the cleverness of a ranch horse outguessing a calf. "Gentle" is another such term, but more literal—a horse which might strenuously object to adult company will nuzzle a toddler's outstretched hand or go willingly for a handicapped rider.

As "Panorama" in the title suggests, this book is intended to offer a view of the wide range of America's horses and ponies and the uses to which they have been put, especially in the present day. Accordingly, chapters on individual breeds and activities are concerned with historical matters only as they bear on contemporary procedures and techniques. Book shops, libraries, and saddlery stores can provide additional reading sources in the event anyone wishes to find out more about any aspect of horses and horsemanship.

Please consider PANORAMA OF AMERICAN HORSES as an invitation to discover (or rediscover) the wealth of equine activities in this country. Try riding, or attend a horse show, rodeo or day (or evening) at the races. The more you see and do, the more you will appreciate subtleties and proficiency involved in all aspects of horsemanship. Moreover, you will find something reassuringly basic about being around horses in this era when technology and overpopulation whittle away at our spirit—"the outside of a horse is good for the inside of a man" puts it well. See for yourself, and you will be the richer for it.

—Steven D. Price

8

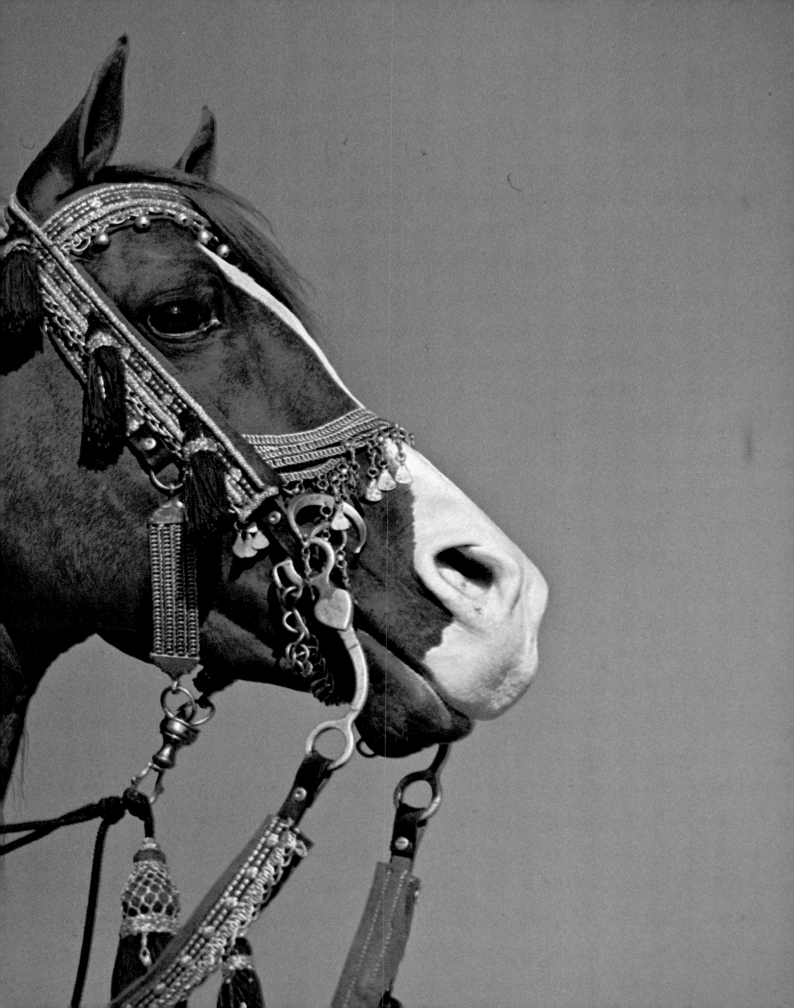

THOROUGHBREDS

Ask a group of people what the word "horse" brings to mind, and it's better than even-money almost everyone's response will be "racing." That association has not only made racing the number one spectator sport in the United States and a billion-dollar business, but has elevated its equine participants to an aristocracy in the world of horses. Those Thoroughbreds involved in the turf as well as other facets of riding have long exhibited qualities of performance, courage and beauty so that the name of the breed has come to stand for the apex of any pursuit.

The story of the Thoroughbred begins with three horses brought from the Middle East to England in the late seventeenth and early eighteenth centuries. Desert breeds of light horses had been sought in western Europe since the Crusades, but few people had the opportunity to own any of these animals which were guarded as closely as any member of a sultan's harem. But a Captain Byerly acquired one in Turkey, sending it back to Britain to stand at stud in the 1680s and 1690s—the Byerly Turk. An English merchant sent another home in 1704, a four-year-old bay colt with a white blaze and stockings which would come to be known as the Darley Arab. The third, the Godolphin Barb, a brown born in 1725 and given to the King of France by the Bey of Tunis, was ultimately sold into the stable of a British nobleman.

Although the reputation of the Eastern horse (the Barb and Turk were similar to, but slightly more coarse than the Arab) lay in its fleetness, none of these three, so far as it is known, ever raced. Their fame came from introducing purer strains into England, a nation whose equine population had become a mélange of assorted types.

How, then, did a new breed of horses come out of this trio? The answer may be found in the mares which they serviced, horses which reflected generations of heavier types. Foals by the Barb, Turk, and Arab were bred back to their dams to retain new characteristics. The product was an animal resembling the desert breeds but perhaps a hand taller and with greater speed. It was this speed which rapidly attracted the attention of sportsmen; a son of the Darley Arab, for instance, beat the best horses of its day over four and six mile distances, and lines of mares formed to be mated to the Arab to obtain the same blood.

Within four generations the basis of the Thoroughbred was

established. Matchem, foaled in 1748, was the grandson of the Godolphin Barb. Born in 1758, Herod was the great-great grandson of the Byerly Turk, as was Eclipse, foaled in 1764, of the Darley Arab. They kept the reputations of the first trio alive and in the process became the foundation sires of the Thoroughbred, to which everyone since then can (and must) trace its ancestry. Each was a stunning performer under saddle—Eclipse was never defeated at any time during its racing career. Each also made its mark as a stud, siring foals out of England's best mares to produce children which bore their conformation and racing ability. What had started as an attempt merely to improve the quality of private owners' horses had revolutionized racing, for the best of this trio's crop was too valuable for anything else than competition on the turf. Thoroughbred thus came to mean race horse.

It was only in the regions of colonial America where the Puritan ethic held sway that racing was not a popular diversion. The first British governor of New York built a track on Long Island where "Dutch" type horses of chunky conformation galloped in quarter-mile contests. Tidewater planters in Virginia and Maryland delighted in matching their animals in dashes down streets and after a day's fox hunting. As soon as it was possible to import Thoroughbreds, colonists did so. Bulle Rock was the first to reach these shores. This son of the Darley Arab and grandson of the Byerly Turk came in 1730 to stand at stud in Virginia. Another was Little Janus, a shade over fourteen hands, whose get were especially apt at quarter-mile races. To obtain the bloodline of one of the foundation sires was worth almost any amount to Virginia sportsmen who showed off their animals. A contemporary account reports: "nothing can be more elegant and beautiful than the horses bred here either for the turf, the field, the road, or the coach . . . even the most indigent person has his saddle-horse, which he rides to every place, for in this country nobody walks on foot the smallest distance."

Diomed was the first of America's important Thoroughbreds. A failure as a racer and sire in England, he was exported to Virginia in 1798. Perhaps the sea voyage improved his constitution, for he turned into a potent stallion until the age of thirty. A son, Sir Archie, was the swiftest of its day, trouncing all comers. From then on, the history of American Thoroughbreds begins to read like a string of Biblical

Swaps

muzzle, while others are fitted with eye cups to reduce their line of vision. The spectator can also see jockeys up close here. The best of these athletes are among the highest-paid in all sport since they receive ten per cent of the owners' share of the purse (or a flat fee for riding horses which finish out of the money). Two features all jockeys share is size, few being taller than a few inches above five feet, and weight. The latter can be a serious problem for some riders who must shed extra poundage to meet their horses' assigned impost (any difference between the assigned weight and the jockey's is made up by pieces of lead carried in the saddle cloth). Most jockeys gravitated toward racing when they realized their diminutive stature, first working as grooms and exercise boys. Riders just starting out, apprentices, are given weight allowances which they shed when they have ridden a certain number of winners. Jockeys wear one of the last vestiges of heraldry in the twentieth century: colored and patterned caps and blouses called "silks" identifying the horse's owner. Some silks date back to the earliest days of American racing, for the turf is often a family tradition. Silks also make it easy to distinguish among Thoroughbreds during a race when the spectator cannot always see saddle cloth numerals.

Once jockeys rode with long stirrups. Now they sit in an exaggerated forward seat, legs tucked under to sacrifice security to reduce wind resistance. As soon as they cross the finish line, they stand in the stirrup irons to slow their horses.

A recent development is the licensing of women jockeys, who bring to the sport the same finesse and sensitivity they have shown in other areas of the horse world.

One of the horses in the paddock strikes the observer's fancy, a big chestnut named Weekend Warrior. Remembering his National Guard service, the observer decides to wager two dollars on a "hunch bet." He gives the horse's program number and his money to a man at one of the "Win" windows in exchange for a ticket which the pari-mutuel machine prints on the spot. (It contains a series of code numerals and letters to prevent forgeries.) On his way to his seat, the spectator notes that the bet wasn't so great a risk; Weekend Warrior's odds are listed at 8-1, third favorite in the race.

The race begins below the grandstand, affording a view of the gate. One animal breaks through the barrier, galloping along until a scarlet-coated outrider intercepts it and returns it to the others. All are finally loaded into their stalls, the starter presses the button, "and they're off!" covering the first few strides in thirty-foot leaps.

The race is at a mile and one-sixteenth. At this distance Weekend Warrior's jockey settles him down toward the rear of the pack, letting three horses set the pace. They do, and at the end of the backstretch the spectator's choice begins to make its move, passing tired horses for the lead. Another horse is also making a bid, and the two race stride for stride until the sixteenth pole. There the other draws ahead and finishes two lengths in front of Weekend Warrior.

The observer is about to discard his ticket when a roar goes up. The tote board has flashed an "inquiry" sign—the possibility of a foul which could affect the race's outcome. It is between Weekend Warrior and the horse which crossed the line first. The riders of both horses are summoned to the stewards' room to watch motion pictures of the race (an instant replay of all stages of the event) and be cross-examined about possible interference. The track announcer tells the crowd to hold onto all tickets until the race is declared official.

Another shout erupts. Evidently the other horse had impeded Weekend Warrior, since the latter's number is posted in first position (jockeys may also claim foul against each other; any rider adjudged guilty of negligence during the course of a race may be suspended for a certain number of days, penalties honored at all Thoroughbred tracks around the country). The observer cashes in his ticket, receiving a little more than $18.00 (8-1 on his $2 bet, plus his original investment). Past performances and bloodlines be hanged is his feeling, but another hunch bet on a horse named after his home town quickly shows him the error in such a "system."

The feature race has attracted some of the best Thoroughbreds in the country, winners of hundreds of thousands of dollars all trying to add this purse to their bankrolls. It is a handicap, meaning the track's racing secretary has assigned unequal weights in an attempt to make the contest fairer. The observer decides, since all the entries look good, to do some handicapping of his own by checking "form" in the racing newspaper. Every detail of a Thoroughbred's racing life is listed: the date and distance of past contests, the weight it carried, the track condition (fast, muddy or sloppy—some animals perform well on "off" tracks, while others prefer a firm footing), how it did

Bold Ruler

57

Jersey. Top Thoroughbreds used are no strangers to racing, since most have competed on flat tracks. Many which could (or would) not excel at even six-furlong sprints have become consistent performers over jumps and at longer distances for reasons they choose to keep to themselves.

There are two types of events. One is over timber—long fences which do not yield to impact. Hurdle races require clearing jumps made of brush, through the tops of which horses can sail. Hurdle races tend to be somewhat shorter than steeplechases (those over timber), or more precisely, the longest steeplechase is longer than the furthest of those over brush. The greater distances—two to four miles —require a more solidly-built Thoroughbred than flat racing, deep in the chest, strong hind quarters, and tough legs to withstand the jolt of landing at a gallop after a four-foot jump. There are other differences, too: greater stamina is required to carry heavier riders and assigned weights, up to 170 pounds. Jockeys ride with longer stirrups for greater security and control, and they may wear spurs (flat jockeys cannot) in addition to carrying crops to urge their mounts.

Jumping races at major tracks do not attract the betting public as less risky contests on the flat do, causing something of a curtailment over the years. But to picnic on a rolling hillside overlooking "fair hunting country" while watching Thoroughbreds competing in this natural setting attracts an increasing number of people every year to steeplechasing.

There are few activities in which the Thoroughbred does not participate. It forms the backbone of international jumping teams, including our own United States Equestrian squad. Individuals' natural physical ability plus boldness and intelligence inherent in the breed make them outstanding for three-day events including dressage and cross-country as well as stadium jumping. Several have cleared in excess of seven feet. They are at home in the show ring's hunter classes, ears pricked forward as they clear the same sort of obstacles found in the hunting field. Thoroughbreds make polo ponies *par excellence*. Having contributed to the creation of the Quarter Horse, Thoroughbreds have successfully competed against them in rodeo and stock-seat events. The center of attention at any riding academy which has one is the Thoroughbred hack, perhaps a little "hot" for a beginner, but an accomplished rider's dream mount.

Watch a horse unconfined by a saddle move around a pasture or paddock. From a standstill it goes into a slow and easy walk, moving its head with every step. Then something can attract its attention. Head held higher, it increases its speed in an effortless, steady, flowing motion, legs still going in a diagonal pattern. It has broken into a trot, one of its natural gaits. Not the fastest (the gallop holds that distinction), but the one a horse uses to cover distance most easily. A trotting horse is an arresting sight, one which led to the production of a breed which capitalizes on the gait. That breed is the Standardbred, the light harness horse.

Among the first horses brought to this country was a type which originated in the Netherlands. Like diminutive versions of the Flemish Great Horse, they were solidly-built animals designed for work. In colonial America, work included transporting a rider under saddle. Centering in New England, their natural propensity for pacing was emphasized, for the lateral movement of that gait was more comfortable over long distances than a trot. It was quite acceptable to use these horses for riding, but racing in the Massachusetts Bay Colony was as morally reprehensible as it had been in Puritan England under Oliver Cromwell's Commonwealth. Settlers who disagreed with the prevailing ethic moved with Roger Williams to establish a more liberal colony in Rhode Island, where one can imagine liberated sportsmen hastening to discover the relative speed of their mounts. These horses were called Narragansett pacers, highly regarded throughout the thirteen colonies. (One of them played an important role in American history as the horse which Paul Revere borrowed for his ride.)

This stallion shows classic Standardbred conformation. Thoroughbred, Morgan and light harness characteristics are evident in the size and shape of the neck, body and legs, the result of breeding for power and ease at pulling a sulky at top trotting or pacing speeds.

With the founding of a new nation, the Thoroughbred reigned supreme as the horse for distance racing. Quarter mile sprints were popular too. That left the pacer in the lurch, so to speak, for it seemed to most people that to race at anything less than a gallop was a waste of time and horseflesh. It took a superlative horse to change this attitude, and one arrived from England in 1788, Messenger, a grey Thoroughbred of the Darley Arab strain. Messenger's value in this country lay in his siring ability. He fathered over 600 foals which grew into well-built animals, many of which showed an aptitude for trotting speedily.

Until the nineteenth century, trotters and pacers had been raced under saddle, riders negotiating the bounces as best they could at the extended gait. It was difficult to urge one's horse ahead while trying to maintain his equilibrium, so someone had the idea to strip a wagon of excess items and drive the animal from behind it. Good horses did not seem to mind the weight. One of the Messenger line, Lady Suffolk, became the first to draw a wagon over a mile in under two and one-half minutes, beating that mark by just one-half a second (Lady Suffolk is better remembered as "The Old Grey Mare" of the folk song.)

Trotting races received new interest when Northern legislatures curtailed Thoroughbred contests, a vestige of the Puritan attitude. But it was difficult to stop a man from matching his carriage horse against another's, and it was a mark of prestige to be seen driving a high-stepping flashy animal. A trotting horse in 1818 drew approval by going from New York to Philadelphia in one day, returning after a few days of rest. After a suitable period of obeisance to "morality," states relented and permitted trotting contests to return.

A great-grandson of Messenger, Hambletonian, was among the most prepotent horses in history. Flourishing after the Civil War, Hambletonian sired more than 1300 foals of which at least forty trotted the mile in under two minutes, 30 seconds. His ancestor's blood was held responsible, and Messenger was later declared the foundation sire of Standardbreds. Blue Bull another stallion of that era but not of Thoroughbred lineage, sired more than fifty children which covered that distance under the mark.

Until Messenger's progeny began to dominate match races and time trials, the Morgan breed was well regarded as a road horse.

Ethan Allen, three generations away from Justin Morgan, once trotted a mile in two minutes, 15 seconds. Although a Morgan's shorter stride could not match descendants of Thoroughbreds, it possessed greater stamina; many of the best Standardbreds can find Morgan infusions in their family trees.

Impetus for trotting racing enthusiasm was never hard to locate. Every family had its horses and light vehicle for transportation, just the combination for seeing whose animal was fastest (and, by implication, which man or boy was most adept at handling the reins and whip). A family driving home from church or town would usually come upon a neighbor. Buggies moved abreast to allow conversation. Bored by small talk, one of the men imperceptibly tried to increase the pace. His neighbor obliged, and before passengers could object, the race was on. Wives shrieked while sons cheered on the combatants who by that time were oblivious to jolts from rocks and ruts in the road. The contest ended when one of the buggies outdistanced its rival, the losing driver slinking home to brood about trading in Old Ned for a faster animal. Small wonder, with all those amateur events, touring professional races were immensely popular at state and county fairs.

One of the best-known horses after the Civil War was Little Brown Jug, a pacer standing under 15 hands. Another was Star Pointer, having the distinction of being the first recorded as covering a mile in under two minutes, doing a spectacular 1:59¼ in 1897.

But no trotter or pacer could demonstrate its maximum speed pulling an albatross of a sulky (riding Standardbreds went out of vogue after the Civil War). Those two-wheeled vehicles in the nineteenth century were uncomfortable, heavy (approximately seventy pounds), and precarious (wheels were over five feet high). Maneuverability, especially around turns, was minimal. But drivers could exercise greater control and horses had less weight to tote when sulkies were built with bent axles and shock-absorbing springs. 1892 saw the introduction of the bicycle wheel, lower and pneumatically cushioned. A bicycle-type seat lowered the driver's center of gravity and cut down wind resistance, also cutting down times of races.

One of the legendary Standardbreds, foaled in 1896, was the pacer Dan Patch, also of the Messenger line. He equaled Star Pointer's record and was unbeaten in three racing seasons, losing only two heats in the process. When there was no one left to beat, Dan Patch toured the country to establish new track records wherever he went. In 1906 behind a galloping horse, he set a mark for the mile in one minute, 55 seconds. The time was disallowed as a record, however, because of the pace-setter, but Dan Patch covered the distance in only one-fourth of a second longer at a later date. One of his drivers speculated that he could have done better; the running horse setting the pace hemorrhaged and seconds were lost by swerving around the animal. Dan Patch had done the three-quarters in one minute, 25 seconds.

All racing slowed down in the early 1900s in a wave of reaction to scandals. Harness racing suffered the additional burden of competition from the automobile's wooing American men away from wheels drawn by horses. Only at fairs and exhibitions did owners and breeders have a chance to perform with their animals.

Another great Standardbred did much to revive the sport. Greyhound trotted his way through the 1930s to ultimately a 1:55¼ record for the mile. (Trotters tend to be somewhat slower than pacers, but ever since a mare named Lou Dillon broke the two-minute barrier in 1903, trotters have had nothing to be ashamed of.)

Any decline ended in 1940 when Roosevelt Raceway on New York's Long Island was the first to present night racing. Patrons flocked to enjoy an evening's entertainment under floodlights at times when they didn't have to play hookey from work. Increasing attendance and tracks' share of betting pools induced more horsemen to enter the sport, from which faster animals resulted. Records fell over the next thirty years, thanks to trotters and pacers such as Rodney, Good Time, Bret Hanover, Bye Bye Byrd, Adios Butler, Su Mac Lad, and Nevele Pride. Sons and daughters of these horses have already begun to challenge their parents' marks for time and money earned.

The "standard" in Standardbred was created to separate those horses which could cover a specific distance within an arbitrary standard, originally set at two minutes, 30 seconds. The registry maintained by the United States Trotting Association lists bloodlines back to Messenger; selective breeding since then has been the primary method of blending disparate types and strains into the Standardbred.

Other breeds have more distinguishing points of conformation than the Standardbred. It resembles the Thoroughbred, but averages somewhat smaller, about 15 hands. Of much the same ancestry as the Quarter Horse, it displays the same sturdy build, although finer in features. Weight varies between 900 and 1,200 pounds. Solid color coats run the spectrum from black to grey, with bay, chestnut, and brown in between.

Because the Standardbred is not ridden, training can begin earlier than for other breeds. Only one day after its birth a foal is fitted with a light halter and led out of, then back to its stall, its dam reassuringly in attendance. The animal thus learns at that tender age to know and trust humans. Breaking to harness begins when the horse is a yearling. It is introduced to a bridle and snaffle bit. Then a girth is fitted, its tightness gradually increased. Taking the horse out of the barn, the trainer attaches long reins to the bridle, showing the yearling how to be driven by walking several yards behind the apprehensive animal; in this manner it learns to become familiar with signals for starting, turning, and stopping.

Being hitched to a training, or jogging cart is the next step. As another man holds a lead line attached to the bridle, the trainer patiently induces the horse to pull the vehicle, somewhat heavier than the sulkies to which it will subsequently be hitched. (Racing sulkies now weigh approximately forty pounds.)

When the Standardbred is capable of drawing the cart on its own (without being led), it spends many miles and weeks developing

requisite muscles and stamina. Round and round the track it goes, in both directions to develop balance. No speed is demanded for quite a while, but when it finally is, the trainer takes pains to make sure his charge does not discover the cardinal sin of any harness horse, breaking into a canter or gallop. To keep a pacer in the correct gait are leather straps called hobbles. Fastened above the knee, they interfere with any leg movement but the required lateral motion. Certain pacers race "free-legged," but few trainers are willing to take the chance of a horse's going off stride in the heat of combat. After jogging comes "brushing," an increase of speed up to a three-minute mile. Then, when a Standardbred demonstrates an ability to perform well enough for competition, it is time to be outfitted for the races.

In addition to a bridle (and hobbles for pacers), the Standardbred wears a harness to which the sulky's shafts are attached. A check rein goes from the top of the girth, separating at the bridle's headpiece and fastened to each side of the cheek strap. Its purpose is to prevent the horse from losing optimum balance by lowering its head. Like some saddle horses, certain Standardbreds require a martingale, another strap which acts against tossing the head. Pacers use shadow rolls as Thoroughbreds do to prevent shying. Another device to keep a pacer on a straight course is the head pole, a rod going from girth to headpiece. Boots provide leg protection, especially against forging, when a trotter's hind leg strikes a foreleg. Forging can also be helped by corrective shoeing. Trotters usually wear heavier shoes than pacers, but in each instance it is a matter of consultation between trainer and blacksmith.

Whether a race program will be held at a rural track redolent with tradition or at a modern complex glowing at night like the city of Oz, there is a relaxed, good-time feeling about going out to watch "the trots." The racing strip is usually a half-mile oval, banked around the turns and manicured for top speeds. Artificial surfaces are becoming popular for their imperviousness to wet weather. Pacing races now tend to outnumber trotting events. Before and during the contests a bevy of harness horses can be seen "scoring," a warm-up procedure normally done twice before a race.

There are several differences between Thoroughbred and Standardbred racing. One which immediately strikes the observer when he checks the program is the smaller number of entrants in harness races. There are seldom more than eight in a field because of the room drivers need to maneuver their sulkies.

Races begin from a moving start. In the old days drivers positioned themselves in any way they could to get a jump on the starter's pistol, leading to many false or off-pace starts. Now a mobile gate is used: entries move up to a barrier mounted across the back of a car, which increases speed until pulling away from the field at the starting line, to permit all to begin at good rate and on stride.

Many drivers are men who also own or train their horses. Weight and age are not factors in this sport, as many compete long after the age when a jockey would have retired. Split-second judgments and reflexes are drivers' stock-in-trade: whether an opening between sulkies is wide enough to pass through or whether it would

A pacer out for a morning's exercise. Hobbles restrict its legs to keep it in the proper gait, while a shadow roll and blinders focus its attention on the matter at hand.

be wiser to move on the outside. A particularly useful skill is how to handle the reins when a horse breaks gait, since galloping too long or at the finish will result in disqualification. Drivers wear distinctive outfits, including protective caps, jackets and trousers bearing their stable's colors. Goggles guard against flying clods of dirt. The men carry whips approximately five feet in length. Their horses bear colored saddlecloths indicating post position and numbered discs of the same colors on their bridles.

Another element of Standardbred racing is that horses must compete against others of similar caliber. Categories start at the fastest, Free For All through the alphabet and numbers from A-1 to D-3. A horse which has shown improvement "moves up in class" to meet new competition, while those with decreasing speeds are dropped back.

Trotting races are conducted along the lines of Thoroughbred racing in most other respects. There are handicaps, but post position, not weights, provide the advantage (a large proportion of horses starting from the inside spot end up as winners, since they have less ground to cover if they stay on the rail). Pari-mutuel betting is of course an attraction. Most tracks have, in addition to win, place, and show wagering, a daily double where a bettor is required to predict the winners of the first and second races before the initial contest.

An exacta calls for selecting the first and second horse in one race in that order. Patrons who bet on a superfecta, the exact order of the first four finishers expect and get large pay-offs—a $2 superfecta bet in June, 1972 at Roosevelt Raceway returned over $16,000. Like Thoroughbred racing, interference with another horse can be grounds for disqualification and/or suspension of the driver.

Trotting races are not confined to the United States. Every year this country plays host to the world's best harness horses. International events, to which foreign trotters and pacers are invited, generally take place at over a mile, since the visitors are used to going greater distances. Nevertheless, American horses are consistently among those in the money.

Top events do not always take place at million-dollar steel-and-glass raceways. Delaware, Ohio is the site of The Little Brown Jug pacing classic for three-year-olds, while The Hambletonian for trotters of that age is held at Du Quoin, Illinois. Goshen, New York, home of the Hall of Fame of the Trotter, is another small town long associated with the sport.

Once upon a time, and not so many years ago, boys in Indiana snuck away from school recess to watch Dan Patch's private railroad car pass through town. Their fathers sat around a stove in the local general store discussing the relative merits of bloodlines and recalling great trotters and pacers of their youth. Harness racing still speaks to something in our past. Perhaps it is because contemporary harness horses still are asked to match or better times set over one hundred years ago. Whether at a county fair or a modern urban complex, the sport touches the past, reverberating with centuries of wheels churning up dirt roads behind straining muscles and the proud pounding of hoofbeats.

QUARTER HORSES

Imagine a ranch scene out West. It's spring and cowboys have brought a herd of cattle down from winter pasture. Among the herd are calves which need to be branded and inoculated, as well as several steers showing signs of illness. To separate them from the others is a job for a specially trained horse yet one also versatile enough to perform all kinds of ranch and range duties. Among Westerners the horse for such a spot has always been the Quarter Horse.

The Quarter Horse arose as a type, one which could trace its ancestry to those animals brought to America by Spanish explorers. Unlike the color breeds arising in the West, however, its forebears were those which escaped or were stolen from conquistadors and colonists who settled east of the Mississippi, especially in what is now Florida, Georgia and South Carolina. In the hands of forest Indians, tough Arab and Barb became the Cherokee and Chickasaw ponies standing about 14 hands high, short legged and able to jump off into a gallop in a flash. As the ponies were introduced in the colonies of North Carolina, Virginia and Maryland, they were bred to English horses of the same general conformation, particularly to chunky Narragansett pacers. Matched against Thoroughbreds, they could get off to a quicker start and lead up to one-fourth of a mile or so, then yielding to their longer-limbed rivals; the shorter animals lacked what horsemen called "bottom," stamina needed to continue at top speed over a greater distance. To distinguish between them and Thoroughbreds, they were called Quarter-of-a-Mile Runners, a phrase shortened to Quarter Horses.

A method of promoting this type of horse was to introduce and interbreed strains of any variety, including Thoroughbreds. One, named Janus, turned out to be initially responsible for establishing Quarter Horses ultimately as a breed. Foaled in 1746, this grandson of Godolphin Barb was brought to Virginia as a six-year-old. Janus could run a four-mile race with the best of them, yet his sons and daughters showed a special aptitude for short dashes. They also tended toward a compact conformation, well-muscled bodies standing between 14 and 15 hands. They and other horses of that type became general utility work animals for harness and farm chores. During off hours they were used for racing.

Quarter mile sprints were popular during and after the Revolu-

Indian cave painting in Arizona chronicle the arrival of Spanish conquistadors and their mounts. The Quarter Horse can trace its ancestry to these animals whose descendants were crossed with Thoroughbred and other breeds. At least two horses in the picture could have been at the root of color breeds family tree, the forerunners of the Pinto.

quarters ready to go in either direction. A good cutting horse gives the impression of a football offensive lineman blocking defenders from reaching the quarterback. The horse should also be able to do the job without any cues from its rider, who can sit in the saddle with his arms folded just watching the spectacle.

Teaching a Quarter Horse its role in calf roping is another product of conditioning. The cowboy initially rides behind a calf while swinging his lasso, in this way accustoming his horse to follow the quarry's movements without being disconcerted by the lasso. The next step is to rope the calf, then signal the horse to stop and backup a few paces. In that way his mount learns to associate a catch with a halt and reverse. Another essential point is that the horse must know to "rate" the calf, staying several yards behind it to allow a clear cast of the rope. Then, when the lasso is wrapped around the saddle horn, the horse is taught to maintain a steady pressure against the rope, which prevents the calf from eluding the then-dismounted roper en route to tying it up. A Quarter Horse's quick starting prowess makes it a perfect partner for this activity; its intelligence and willingness make it a pleasure to school.

Although not all horses were tapped for such specialization, any Western horse had to learn to respond to subtle signals from its rider. Rather than direct, tight pressure on the bit to cue it to turn, the cow pony switched direction by neck-reining, one-handed pressure done with a slack rein. Another all-purpose necessity was stopping on a dime when the rider hopped off.

Quarter Horse conformation was an asset in ranch work, trail riding and sprint racing. The head is short and broad, with strong jaws useful for grazing when grass is in short supply. Ears are small in proportion to the head. The neck is set on lower than most breeds, keeping the center of gravity closer to the ground. A broad, deep chest is the mark of a horse with plenty of room for heart and lungs. The combination of sloping shoulders and high withers is more than useful for keeping a saddle in place, as is the short back. Short cannons on the forelegs contribute to the Quarter Horse's power.

Horses are rear-engined vehicles and it is that portion of the Quarter Horse's anatomy which radiates with power. The rear quarters are deep and muscled down through the legs. As previously noted, the hind quarters are higher than at the withers. Feet and hooves are well-formed, noticeably free from ailments.

Height averages at 15 hands and weight between 1,100 and 1,300 pounds in the mature horse. Solid coats of all colors are usual and a matter of personal preference, bringing to mind a cowboy saying that "a good horse is *any* color." A well-conformed Quarter horse gives the impression of balance and durability, an alert and willing creature.

Development of the breed has continued through this century. The King Ranch in southern Texas has always been one of the great centers of such activities, testing its horses under ranching conditions. Its owners, the Kleberg family, created a new strain of beef cattle and worked just as assiduously toward adapting Thoroughbred stock to become utility cow ponies. The prototype was a horse known as The Old Sorrel sired by a son of Dan Tucker out of a Thoroughbred mare (sorrel is the Western term for the chestnut color). By using The Old Sorrel as a foundation stud and by carefully selecting which of its get would be interbred, the Klebergs produced a crop of horses outstandingly suited for ranch work. A descendant of The Old Sorrel, Wimpy, was chosen as the first horse to be admitted to registry by the American Quarter Horse Association.

Although people had known for over two hundred years that there was a Quarter Horse or at least a type, it was not until 1940 that a breeding organization was established. The American Quarter Horse Association determined conformation standards and in 1941 opened a registry. It is proud of the fact that more than 50,000 new horses a year are added, the total now in the area of 600,000.

The breed's racing activities have come a long way from sprints down a colonial street with bales of tobacco going to the winner's owner. Quarter Horses had always been involved in races, both these impromptu ones as well as others more planned, but they lacked the supervision and regulations which the Thoroughbred part of the sport enjoyed. A judge who made an unpopular decision could be tarred and feathered, while a losing jockey frequently left town faster than he moved during the race. All this changed in 1941. Under the aegis of the American Quarter Horse Association, tracks opened around the country, including Los Alamitos, California, Lafayette, Louisiana, and Raton and Ruidoso, both in New Mexico.

Like Standardbred trotters and pacers, Quarter Horse racers are rated into classes based on their speed. The fastest time category

*As sure-footed as the mules
which follow, this Quarter
Horse moves a pack train high
above the timber line of
Glacier Peak, Washington.*

is Top AAA for horses which can run a quarter of a mile in less than 22.1 seconds. Next is AAA for between 22.11 and 22.5 seconds down to D, a "sluggish" 24.11 or more. All horses must be registered with the breed's association and the divisions are based on their carrying 116 pounds. One-fourth of a mile is the maximum distance Quarter Horses are asked to run, but there are also events at 220, 250, 300, 350 and 400 yards.

Few people outside the sport are aware that the richest purse in all of horse racing is for this breed. Held every Labor Day at Ruidoso Downs, the event is the All-American Futurity at 440 yards. Earlier qualifying heats determine which are the ten entrants for a total prize in excess of $600,000. The record time is 19.09 seconds, which gives some indication of how a Quarter Horse race is run. There is no jockeying for position—from starting gate to finish line the name of the game is speed. Hundredths of seconds separate the finishers, over all of which a not-very-large blanket could be draped at the wire.

Most of the classes for Quarter Horses at shows revolve around the breed's ranching background. Accordingly, Western tack—curb bits or hackamores and stock saddles—are required, and riders must wear ten-gallon hats and high-heeled boots (and chaps in working classes). Reins must be held in one hand. A reining class takes place in an arena approximately 150 by 50 feet. The horse's responsiveness is at issue, manifested by effortless performance through mandatory figures, something of a Western dressage event. It may begin with a gallop for twenty feet, followed by a halt and rein back, several figure-eights and pivots, and standing for inspection. Like dressage, an entrant is judged on naturalness and ease of motion, losing points when the rider is forced to exert too much control or give cues in too obvious a fashion.

Western Riding Horse classes simulate activities a Western horse encounters at work. Horses are shown at a walk, trot and lope in both directions, as well as over or through obstacles. The latter includes opening, riding through, then closing a gate and passing over four logs and a wooden bridge. Other things for a horse to do may be a water hazard to cross, backing, entering a trailer and being led on foot over obstacles. As in ranch work or pleasure riding, the horse must display good manners and a willingness, together with an easy-going, reliable manner of moving.

Quarter horses also appear under English tack in jumping, English pleasure, and polo classes. They are especially adept at the last, as well as actually doing the sport, thanks to their ability to start, stop, and change directions so rapidly.

The era of old-style ranching is over. Cattle are now taken to market in trucks, no longer taken across country on trail drives. Horses share stabling facilities with jeeps and helicopters used for transportation and during round-ups. Yet the Quarter Horse is no anachronism. No helicopter can get close enough to rescue a steer trapped in a stand of timber, nor is four-wheel drive of great value in cutting a calf from a herd. But its use as a cow pony does not entirely explain why the Quarter Horse is America's fastest-growing breed. Ask anyone who has owned or ridden one. Beneath its hardy exterior is an animal willing to learn and eager to please. It takes to seemingly-impassable terrain as handily as it provides an amiable trail ride for dude ranch tenderfeet. Since very few equestrians have the opportunity or inclination for long distance galloping, the Quarter Horse can be all things to all riders. Spectators appreciate its speed in racing and versatility as rodeo and show performers. Originating in the East, then moving to the West, the Quarter Horse continues to be a true representative of the entire United States.

Enjoying an outing in South Carolina attests to the nationwide popularity of Quarter Horses.

104

COLOR
BREEDS

Surveying horses in America raises the question of what makes a breed a breed. The word is most commonly used to describe a group of individuals which share certain characteristics, which in turn define their collective uniqueness. These traits, which include conformation and inclination toward certain kinds of performance, are perpetuated by breeding only those animals which display them. As such features reappeared among succeeding generations, criteria were established and genealogies compiled by organizations formed to keep tabs on the purity of the breeding, the procedure being called "registration." At some stage a registry is "closed," which means that no foal may be eligible for listing unless both its parents have been registered. At the point a registry is closed a breed is said to exist officially.

Some features are easier to perpetuate than others. Equine size and general conformation are genetically rather predictable, just as two humans are likely to have children of the same body types. The outcome becomes more chancy, however, when coloration is a criterion. Chromosomes controlling hue, it seems, are harder to figure out, which raises a problem with respect to the Pinto, Appaloosa, and Palomino—America's color breeds. Some authorities would contend that it is to beg the question to call them breeds; they are merely types because the colors also appear in "true" breeds, pointing to palomino Saddle Horses and pinto Quarter Horses. Moreover, the degree of controlling these markings is less than the characteristics of, for example, a Thoroughbred or Morgan. Those who contend that the three are indeed breeds acknowledge the difficulties, but feel that there is sufficient uniformity among horses displaying the features to warrant the word. Whether they are "breeds" or "types" is less important for our purposes than the history and present use of such animals. And it is through the history of the horse in the American West that we can trace the rise of the Pinto, Appaloosa, and Palomino.

"Goodbye Old Paint" begins a well-known cowboy song and can introduce the Pinto, for that breed has been known as paint, skewbald, piebald and other names reflecting its coat patterned with patches and spots. Marked horses have been found in many breeds, including the light Arabs and Barbs which Spanish explorers and settlers brought to the New World. Indians immediately took a fancy to the spotted animals.

(opposite) A Pinto trained and posed for saddle seat competition.
(left) A Pinto crossed with Quarter Horse for Western stock work.

111

Legend has it that horses which strayed away from Spanish settlements rapidly populated the Western plains, providing mounts for Indians, but it was, in fact, a slow procedure. Europeans realized that the ownership of horses was an advantage and passed strict laws forbidding selling them to Indians. But many animals were conveniently "lost" or stolen away by stableboys, turning up miles away in native villages. Although any horse was a welcome addition, those with markings were especially prized since the patterns were in keeping with traditional designs which were an integral part of the Indian culture.

The spread of horses among Indians began in the Southwest, among Kiowa and Apache tribes around 1600. They acquired the animals by trade, purchase or theft (horse-stealing was an honorable pursuit to Indians, while the regulations against Spaniards' dealing in horses were suspended to recapture runaway slaves for which Indians insisted on horses in return). It took many years to create a herd. A drought or blizzard could decimate the ranks, and a famine might necessitate a diet of horsemeat. But from the Kiowa and Apache to the Blackfeet and Crow over one hundred years later, almost every Western tribe obtained and became dependent on the horse.

A buffalo hunter once had to lie in ambush until his prey wandered into arrow range. Mounted, however, he could pursue, galloping alongside to permit a clear shot. The horse also became a beast of burden, for transportation in the seasonal migrations to follow buffalo herds, pulling sled-like travois faster than dogs or humans could. So important was the horse to the Indian that it was regarded as a member of the family; some spent bitter nights inside the teepee while a hapless son was ordered to sleep outside. Indians tended to treat their horses more kindly than Spaniards when it came to riding. Instead of cruel bits and back-breaking saddles, Indians used loose-rope hackamores or leather straps attached to the lower jaw and sat bareback or on blankets. Guidance came primarily from knee pressure and voice commands, freeing the rider's hands for the bow and arrow.

Those of us weaned on Saturday afternoon shoot-em-ups saw hundreds of Indians racing around wagon trains and biting the dust under a hail of white men's bullets. Such scenes are pure Hollywood,

for the mounted warrior was a skillful and formidable figure. In battles with other tribes where the goal was not to kill but merely to touch an opponent with a coup stick, he moved with the speed of a light dragoon and the maneuverability of a snake. To capture an opponent's horse was a mark of valor, with spotted animals a great prize. Few tribes did not adorn their horses with war paint as well as to themselves. A naturally spotted horse eliminated the problem of sweat and dirt washing away the decorations, for it carried its own, nature-bestowed symbols of victory. (An animal of any color which proved its value as a warhorse was given ceremonial markings as a reward.)

Horses of less (or more) than solid coats were appreciated by cowboys for the simple aesthetic reason that they looked pretty. Westerners called a white horse with black markings a piebald, and white with markings of any other color a skewbald, both generically termed Paint or Pinto. The latter, a Spanish word for "painted," is how the breed is now officially named. When Pintos were bred to each other, dominant and recessive genes being what they are, the get was not always multicolored, but when it was, a Paint foal might fetch a better price than a plain ol' bay or dun.

Pintos are now separated into two types based on their markings' "direction," overo or tobiano. The white area of the former spreads up from the underside with irregular edges; manes and tails are colored. The tobiano has a white back, mane and tail, and frequently leg markings. Stated more simply (with all the attendant oversimplification), the overo is black (or brown, roan, etc.) with white, while the tobiano is white with colored patches. In neither category are the white areas free from smaller spots or dabs of color. The Pinto can be of any size, although medium (approximately fifteen hands) is the most preferred. Other points of conformation include a smallish head, a short back, deep chest and well-muscled legs. The breed is ridden in both Western and English tack, although the former lends itself to the animals' traditional association with cowboys and Indians. It is exhibited in English, Western and conformation classes; some shows have Pinto Indian costume classes where riders are resplendent in feathered headdresses and other regalia (unlike their ancestors, the horses may not be daubed with color). More informally, Pintos are a colorful and handy addition to any pleasure

the Thoroughbred Denmark and a mare of no particular pedigree. Named Gaines' Denmark, he stood out both for his gaits and conformation, the latter including an arched neck and tail. Gaines' Denmark also demonstrated a prepotency rivaling that of Justin Morgan, as he sired hundreds of foals which later showed the same propensities of action and physique as their father and grandfather (in fact, Denmark was declared foundation sire of the American Saddle Horse). Other animals were chosen for Saddle Horse training and breeding, since there was a tendency for them to pass along their inclination toward easy movements.

The American Saddle Horse, the product of this selectivity, is a possessing creature. Standing from fourteen to sixteen hands, it can range in color from browns and blacks to greys and palomino. A long, graceful neck is set on a well-formed body and lithe legs, but despite this svelte appearance, there is a look of stamina about the breed. This was the horse for the Southern gentleman, capable of an honest day's labor carrying him around his plantation, then displaying a charm and finesse to match the ante-bellum splendor of a stately mansion with portico and columns. It was a sight to bring a whistle of admiration from the mint julep set or to catch the eye of a Scarlett O'Hara.

Depending on their size and aptitude, Saddle Horses are trained for either three- or five-gaited events of horse shows. The three-gaited performs at the natural movements of all horses, the walk, trot and canter. "Five-gaited" refers to these three, plus the slow gait (also known as the singlefoot or stepping pace) and rack. The last mentioned, artificial gaits, evolved from the breed's pacer forebears. As one can see in certain Standardbreds, a horse paces when it moves its two legs on the same side to strike the ground simultaneously. It is a rapid gait, but the twisting motion tended to give a rider the feeling, over an extended period of time, of something approaching seasickness. Therefore, certain pacers were schooled to do the "fox trot," breaking up the leg movements so that the hind foot would strike an instant before the diagonal front hoof. Further refinement turned the fox trot into the slow gait. People find this gait most agreeable, moving easily to the horse's gently rocking movement, as each hoof hits the ground individually but in a syncopated fashion. The rack may be thought of as a fast slow gait since it employs the same leg pattern,

A Tennessee Walking Horse, bred for comfort and style.

era when no day was complete without a drive through the park.

In the broad category of saddle horses (lower case) is the Tennessee Walking Horse. This breed developed, like their Saddle Horse kin, from those Thoroughbreds, Morgans, and pacers brought to the middle Tennessee region. The foundation sire has been determined to be a Standardbred named Black Allen, while other early ancestors include Copperbottom, a Thoroughbred-pacer mix, and Free and Easy, highly admired by so avid a horse fancier as Andrew Jackson.

What sets the Walker (the breed's nickname) apart from the Saddle Horse is its unique gaits, the predilection for which has become hereditary. Its flat-footed walk is an even, balanced action, while the running walk is a four-beat movement during which the animal's hind legs overreach its forelegs' prints sometimes by more than a foot. There is much shoulder motion at the running walk, but little if any swaying. (Form is all-important, and the rules specify that any animal which does not exhibit a straight motion must be disqualified.) Walkers nod their heads at each step of this gliding gait which once carried plantation owners for miles at a clip. The canter is often described as "rocking chair," collected and rolling, so easy to sit to. These are all natural movements, refined by schooling. At one time trainers went to almost any lengths to try to achieve the desired

effects on Walking Horses. They fitted the horses with chains, boots and abrasive chemicals designed to torment the animals in the name of beauty. No such cruelty is now tolerated, and the rules state that irritations or scars on the hoof area, altered hooves, and boots with abrasive substances require disqualification. Further to insure against such practices, all horses in all classes must be inspected by the judge and a veterinarian. Boots are removed and checked, and care is taken to see that no groom or handler substitutes equipment. The rider may not even dismount without official permission. Scrupulous adherence to these regulations has done much to improve the reputation of Tennessee Walkers.

Even conformation is rather strictly outlined. The perfect horse should have a neat, well-shaped head and a neck like the Saddle Horse, long and graceful. The body should be deep at the girth and the legs well muscled. Height ranges between fifteen and sixteen hands, and weight from 1,000 to 1,200 pounds.

Unlike the more testy Saddle Horses, Walkers are delightful for pleasure riding in both English and Western styles. People who have owned or ridden them are quick to sing praises to their amiable temperament, responsiveness, and agreeable gaits—pleasure horses in every sense of the word.

ARABIANS

If this book had been organized according to American horse breeds' importance, the Arabian would be chapters in front of the rest of the field. No other breed has had such an impact on this country (as well as the rest of the world), not so much for its direct participation as for the contributions made in establishing and influencing so many other breeds.

Arabians (the term for individuals; the breed is, properly, the Arab, but the words are used interchangeably) were the first horses brought to the New World, their strains mixed with other types to form the mounts which carried Spanish conquistadors throughout the Southwest in search of cities of gold. These horses took as well to sandy, arid expanses as their purebred forebearers did in the Near East and north Africa, the regions which were the cradle of light horses as well as civilization. Tribesmen held their animals in high esteem, surrounding their origin with quasi-mysticism: the people believed that the first of the breed had been bestowed by the angel Gabriel to Ishmael, son of Abraham. As a means of daily transportation (which included hostilities against other tribes), the Arab excelled at speed and maneuverability, but a far more essential characteristic was endurance. Both men and animals lived in an environment of little food and less water, where an entire day's trip across rock and sand to the next oasis was not unusual. This precarious and nomadic existence left its stamp on the Arab. Lack of nourishment contributed to forming a small stature and slender conformation, the ability to live off small amounts of food, and an extraordinary hardiness. Horses' constant proximity to man and the interdependence which grew between them led to a high degree of domestication; the animals developed intelligence, responsiveness, and good manners which any biped could envy.

The fame of the Arab spread as Europeans discovered the breed during the Crusades and as the armies of Islam moved across Africa into Spain. The art of Spain's "Golden Age" reflected Moorish equine influence; kings and grandees were painted astride purebreds and others crossed with heavier types, the variety of horses explorers and settlers took with them. Europeans in America tried to keep a close watch on their animals, but many were appropriated by Indians or else disappeared into the hills to form bands of wild mustangs.

Arab blood was also introduced by British colonists, whose

135

ancestors had used it to create Hackneys, Welsh Mountain ponies and, of course, the Thoroughbred. It was not, however, until shortly before the Revolutionary War that a purebred Arabian crossed the Atlantic. Named Ranger, the grey stallion stood at stud in Hartford, Connecticut. Its progeny provided mounts for a local regiment, capturing the attention of George Washington. A Captain Lindsay was dispatched to buy it, after which it went to Virginia. Washington bred his own mares to "Lindsay's Arabian" to obtain riding and race horses.

There was at least one other horse with such blood in Connecticut during the latter years of the eighteenth century, for it sired Justin Morgan, progenitor of the breed which bears his name. The stamina, intelligence, and willingness of the Morgan are obviously a heritage from its paternal line. It is difficult now to determine the extent of Arab-types in early America, but the terms "Thoroughbred," "Barb," "blood horse" or "English horse" were employed to mean animals with infusions of desert strains.

Other breeds also owe many of their qualities to Arab stock. The Quarter Horse's Thoroughbred blood rejoined that of the West's

An Arab leads this procession of women dressed in nineteenth century Hawaiian riding habits.

Under saddle or in harness, this breed continues the tradition of endurance and versatility begun by Justin Morgan. A statue to the foundation sire's memory stands in Middlebury, Vermont.

Up to this point we have been concerned with "hot blooded" breeds, a term which describes those horses which developed in the subtropical areas of Arabia and North Africa. These Arabs and Barbs were small in stature, possessed of great speed, and, as if constant exposure to the torrid sun affected their temperament, high spirited. The horses passed along these characteristics in varying degrees to their descendants, characteristics which were sought after by breeders who refined and mixed them according to personal preferences and needs. But another strain of horse arose in northern Europe in areas where nature endowed the animals with large physiques and a hardiness to endure rougher climates. These are the "cold blooded" breeds, as useful to man now in peace as they once were on the battlefield, celebrated for their ability to pull huge weights as draft horses.

All breeds of draft horses descended from the European Great Horse, a type of equine man-of-war which carried knights in full armor through the Middle Ages and Renaissance until the advent of gunpowder eliminated their effectiveness. Size and force were essential elements in the days of plate and chain mail, spears and shields, where the chivalric battleplan was one of little subtlety. Two opposing forces galloped at each other as fast as their horses, carrying up to 400 pounds of man and metal, could go, like football linemen after the snap, on a collision course. The winner was that force with the greater number of survivors; on a personal level, survival meant to remain mounted after an impact or, if unseated in the mêlée, to avoid

(preceding page) A hitch of Clydesdales goes through its paces at a stock show. A Percheron mare with foal bringing up the rear.

160

being trampled by horses, stabbed by wandering squires while lying helpless as a turtle on his back, or just expiring from the heat. Medieval tales about mail-clad knights casually leaping into the saddle were less truth than poetry, since it actually required a winch device to hoist a man aboard. Not only did the Great Horse have to tote such a burden, but the load included plate armor for the animal too. Nevertheless, such was the strength of these chargers that they could move at a respectable gallop.

Flanders was the breeding center for these war steeds (known as Flemish Horses), highly prized from Britain to Italy. William the Conqueror brought several to England to participate in his invasion; they were mated to the largest of the horses left by the Romans, which produced the English Great Horse. Clydesdales developed in the Scottish Lowlands through selective breeding. Back on the Continent the Flemish Great Horse became the Belgian, while in France he was crossed with lighter breeds to become the Percheron. These are the breeds subsequently imported to America where they figured so prominently in the economic and social history of this country as draft horses.

The word 'draft' comes from a verb meaning 'to pull,' and that was the animals' activity even during the time when their brethern served knights in armor. They were not used exclusively at first in this country to haul settlers' wagons and pull plows; oxen were favored (one of the reasons for the preference was their edibility when all other sources of food was unavailable). But oxen's steps were short, and so European heavy breeds were imported to speed pioneers' travels and then finish the day's plowing before sunset.

The first Percherons came to the United States in 1839. Although not much taller than Thoroughbreds (averaging seventeen hands high, but weighing about 2,000 pounds), they made excellent draft horses. Percherons reveal their light horse blood in their clean limbs, fine featured faces, and the clean action of their gaits. Grey or black is the prevalent color, making it relatively easy to match them as a four-in-hand coach hitch. Percherons make up most of the "rosin-back" circus horses, trotting steadily and willingly while acrobats scamper on and vault off their broad backs.

The Belgian arrived on these shores shortly after the Civil War. As befitting these descendants of the Flemish Great Horse, they are the heaviest of the modern draft breeds, often in excess of 2,200 pounds. They carry their bulk well, lifting their chunky legs just enough to clear the ground. Belgians are also recognizable by their light brown color with white markings on fetlocks, mane, and faces, and the tendency toward Roman noses. At one time the Belgian was just another draft breed, but now it is the most popular, in terms of breed registration.

The Clydesdale is something of a showman. Its high-stepping action calls attention to the clumps of hair, called feathers, adorning its fetlocks. Coming to America in the 1870's, they were an attractive addition to a family's stable, pulling coaches and carts in teams of four and eight. It is a relatively light animal, under 2,000 pounds and seventeen hands high. Millions of Americans know the breed because of the famous Budweiser team which draws the beer wagon in television commercials and on personal appearances in parades and fairs across the country.

One also sees members of two other breeds, the Shire and the Suffolk. The former, tall at seventeen hands, was bred specifically as a farm horse, as was the Suffolk, smallish in stature. Both proved excellent workers, but never caught on in this country the way other draft breeds did.

Until the internal combustion engine took over America's roads and acreage, the draft horse was an all-important fixture in urban and rural areas. They were attached to vehicles and plows by stout leather harnesses of which the central feature was a cushioned yoke fitting over the horses' broad shoulders. A well-trained plowing team responded to voice commands to pull, turn in either direction, and stop, but docility and endurance were common to almost all work horses. Now that diesel motors have carried the field and highway, the role of the heavy horse is confined to its influence on certain types of fox hunting mounts (many of the best hunters count a draft horse as one or more of its great-grandparents) and as contestants in county and state fairs pulling events. The burden in these contests is in the form of a dynamometer, a device attached to a truck to measure dead pull. To witness a team urged on by its driver straining against this seemingly immovable object is a thrilling sight, all the more so when the equivalent weight successfully hauled is announced. Events are divided according to animals' weight, and a rule of thumb is that a

spectacular team can pull up to and in excess of its combined weight. For example, two Percherons weighing 2,980 pounds once set a record with a draw of 3,225 pounds, 245 more than their combined weight. In 1937 a pair of Belgians tipping the scales at 4,260 pounds set a heavyweight division mark when they pulled the equivalent of 3,950 pounds.

At another part of the fairground, draft horses may be the subject of critical scrutiny in conformation classes. There judges measure size, build, and markings against standards, awarding ribbons to those which most closely approximate the "perfect" example of Clydesdale, Percheron, Belgian, and other breeds. Whether in harness or standing proudly, draft horses continue to evoke an era whose legacy is the word horsepower, when it stood for the true measure of an animal's utilitarian value to man.

*The Belgian evokes images of
the Flemish Great Horse,
steed of the knight in armor.*

PONIES

The word "pony" means different things to different people. Any horse used for polo, even a seventeen hands high Thoroughbred, is called a pony, but that's a matter of convention. A horse of any breed on the smallish side can be termed a pony, too, but the proper definition is any of several breeds of horses naturally diminutive in size, measuring up to a height of fourteen and one-half hands. There are dozens of pony breeds around the world, but only a few have taken root in the United States. Ponies are used in this country for a variety of activities, pleasure riding, jumping and hunting, and driving.

There is in some circles an antipathy to ponies. They are vicious, malicious and impossible to train, people have said. Besides, their gaits are choppy and a rider's legs drag along the ground. This attitude, however, represents an adult's viewpoint, and is certainly not shared by those of us who had the advantage of growing up around ponies. It may be true that there are some bad apples, but the same may be said of any breed or size (or species, for that matter). Many horsemen recall with great fondness the first time they were hoisted onto the back of a kind, long-suffering Shetland or Welsh Mountain pony. Since the size of a pony is more proportional to a child, ponies can make this initial encounter a good experience, and the friendship can ripen while the young rider learns about hands, seat, and caring for animals. All this is saying no more than if the same care and knowledge is used to select a pony as a horse, the result can be an affectionate and willing addition to the stable and the family.

The Shetland is the most popular pony breed in the United States. Shetlands are immediately recognizable by their size and conformation, seldom if ever growing above twelve hands high, or weighing over 500 pounds. Classic build includes a well-arched neck, a strong, well-rounded body, and short but sturdy legs. Hair runs the spectrum of equine hues and combinations, with manes and tails on the long side, the latter sometimes reaching the ground. Shetlands developed on the rugged, spare island of the same name located 200 miles off the northern coast of Scotland, to which descendants of Roman occupation horses somehow migrated. (Another theory has it that the ponies stem from Scandinavian stock, since the island was once a fief of Iceland.) The lack of abundant food made its mark

Ponies are ubiquitous in the world of horses, appearing wherever their larger brethren do—out hunting, in show rings, and as pleasure mounts. (opposite page, lower right). The high-stepping Hackney in repose.

Young riders exhibit a practiced eye on Connemara (opposite right) and Welsh Mountain ponies.

on succeeding generations, stunting size but forcing them to become tough enough to endure rough winds, rain, and snow. The small stature has made Shetlands ideal for children, and perhaps the Caledonian durability accounts for their tolerance for human horseplay and those errors coming from beginning riders. On the other hand, ponies' reputations as recalcitrant beasts can come in part from their reaction to such abuse; more often than not it is the pony's decision, not his frustrated rider's, to return to the stable or retire to the center of the ring when it has had enough for one day.

The Shetlands' somewhat choppy gaits for riding coupled with their hardiness make them excellent animals for working in harness. They are shown pulling roadsters like miniature Standardbreds or buggies. Brilliance and good manners are judged, so that any ponies who have demonstrated their detractor's criticisms for sloth or ill-temper are not in evidence.

Welsh Mountain ponies developed under similar circumstances to Shetlands, but their development took place in the mountainous area in Western England. As the ponies became domesticated, breeders infused Thoroughbred and Hackney strains, increasing the ponies' size to between eleven and twelve hands and up to 600 pounds. These additions are also evident in Welsh Mountain conformation, especially the longish neck and rump and well-formed legs. Grey is the color most frequently appearing. Welsh Mountain ponies are somewhat more comfortable to ride than Shetlands, and they make excellent mounts for cross-country and trail riding. Inheriting the skill from their forebears, Welsh Mountain ponies, like other small breeds, are at home in hilly terrain, able to negotiate treacherously steep areas in a more sure-footed fashion than larger mounts. On the flat, over jumps or in harness, Welsh Mountain ponies are sturdy and bold performers, either as purebreds or as part of a crossbreed.

179

Ireland is represented in this pony Union Jack by the Connemara. It is the largest of the breeds popular in this country, almost always approaching the limit of 14.2 hands. Its appearance is easy to describe—it looks like a diminutive Thoroughbred, with well-chiseled head, slim legs, and a sloping body. This conformation makes it a good hunter-type, and the ponies seem to recognize this fact. They are bold, clean jumpers. One, for example, competed among larger horses and often defeated them when it cleared seven feet. With such an aptitude for altitude, together with customary sure-footedness, the Connemara is a sure candidate for the hunting field, carrying young and lightweight foxchasers over mile after mile with enough stamina left to be in at the kill. The only facet of the horse world in which the Connemara is not noted as a participant is in harness, but even there several have acquitted themselves well.

Think of ponies and harness, however, and Hackney comes to mind. Completing the Union Jack, this breed grew up in England, the product of Welsh ponies crossed with Arabians and Thoroughbreds. Theirs was not a heritage of scrounging for an available clump of grass; Hackneys grew up under relatively luxurious conditions, and rewarded their owners by providing a variety of services. The word hack, meaning a horse for a pleasure ride, comes from their name, in turn derived from an Anglo-Saxon word "to neigh." Although a fine utility breed, Hackneys showed a disposition to trot and they became light carriage horses. They willingly pulled milady's surrey through a morning's outing in the park or en route to an afternoon's shopping, attracting the attention of spectators wherever they went.

Hackneys still do. Their contemporary careers are pretty much limited to the show ring where they draw, singly or in tandem, light buggies as well polished as their own coats. Even those members of an audience who look askance at such "functionless" events as saddle horses and harness horses find themselves captivated by the diminutive but high-stepping entries. When they appear in pairs, they must be matched within one-half inch in size without losing points, and in those classes where size is a criterion (e.g., between 13 and 14.2 hands) more than one-half an inch will result in disqualification. Exhibited with a short braided mane and tail, they display their fine action at the slower "Park Pace" and the smart trot introduced by the

A Shetland's flowing mane and tail match the landscape's foliage.

181

announcer's command "Show Your Pony." The "heavy artillery" in the Hackney world comes when Four-in-hands are shown. There a stage coach pulled by four ponies carrying at least one man in coaching livery is judged on performance and appointments (the latter must include, as esoteric but as useful an item as a hunter's sandwich box, an umbrella basket).

Since this book is about American breeds, we can look with pride on at least one native strain of pony. When a man in Iowa crossed an Appaloosa with a Shetland, the result was an animal which looked like a cross between an Arabian and a Quarter horse, but with Appaloosa markings. It will take several more generations and greater exposure to determine whether this breed, the Pony of the Americas, will find as great acceptance and use in this country as have its British cousins.

A horse owner or rider can enjoy the sport as a casual pastime, riding alone or going out hacking with a group of friends. But when his thoughts turn to matching his own or his animal's abilities against those of others, the dimension of competition, the heart of any sport, is added. Shows are the proving grounds for such tests of skills, offering events as varied as the types of activities which horses can provide.

Size and formality of shows depend on available facilities and financial resources. Most riding academies have one or two a year for their students and boarders, single-day events beginning in the morning and lasting as long as there are entrants, usually until late afternoon. Others, held either indoors or outside, may last over a weekend, attracting exhibitors from all over a region. The largest shows are week-long fixtures open only to those who during the year have qualified in other shows to be able to compete against the best practitioners of the art of horsemanship, also offering exhibitions such as musical rides by mounted units of a city police force, a Roman-style chariot race, or a team of draft horses pulling a brilliantly polished beer wagon (complete with Dalmatian perched alongside the driver). Shows may be limited to certain breeds, as in, for example, the National Morgan Show in Northampton, Massachusetts, but the majority are showcases for all types and breeds of horses and styles of riding. Duration and prestige, however, have no bearing on the aspiration or perspiration of competitors—a novice performing in a small, dusty ring is subject to the same preparation, tensions, and exuberance over victory (and frustration over mishap or disappointment over losing) as a professional horseman vying for a championship stakes on the tanbark of Madison Square Garden's National Horse Show.

The role of determining excellence falls to judges, many of whom were once exhibitors and all possess a high degree of expertise and experience, particularly in areas like conformation and equitation where their subjectivity is the sole criterion. They are certified by the American Horse Show Association after their qualifications have been attested to by interested members of the equestrian community. In addition to specific factors in the diverse kinds of classes, judges in turn look for good sportsmanship, character, and courtesy toward mounts and other exhibitors and, in equitation

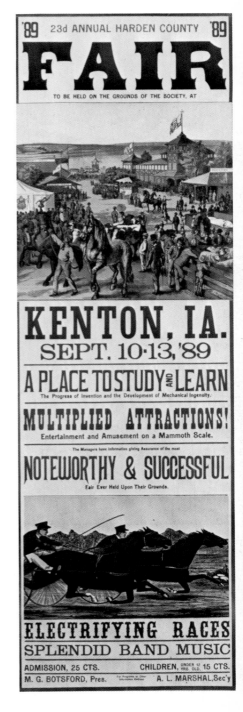

187

riders, and onlookers. Experts design courses to test both power and maneuverability, placing obstacles (of the same kind as those in equitation classes) of varying heights, widths, and spreads around the ring. Size, however, is not the sole factor; the course should be a fair test of a well-schooled jumper's ability. Scoring depends on the conditions of the class. One mishap and you're finished in the demanding Knockdown-and-Out, the winner being the one who clears the greatest number of fences without a fault. In events where touches count, a brush by a horse's forelegs is given one-half fault, and by its hind legs one fault, while a knockdown is penalized by four faults. Refusal results in three faults for the first, six for a second, and elimination in the event of a third (elimination is also the penalty for going off course or falling). A class gaining in popularity is the exciting "Gambler's Choice": each obstacle is given a point value depending on its difficulty and riders may jump them in whatever order they choose to build up the highest score, all within a time limit. Time is a factor in other jumping events, encouraging riders to cut corners to shave precious seconds while trying to make sure their mounts take off and land in balance, no easy task when around a sharp turn may lie a five-foot spread. In the event there are tie scores, there are additional rounds called jump-offs, where fences are raised. Certainly the most hair-raising of open jumping classes is the Puissance. Obstacles begin at four and one-half feet and can reach over seven in jump-offs. The sight of a finalist approaching a "great wall" will bring the crowd to silence, and should he clear it the neighborhood will resound with shouts of released tension.

The blare of the ringmaster's coach horn heralds a flight of harness horses. They are as elegantly turned out as their drivers, women wearing long skirts. After the rigs have trotted around the ring, the judge passes down the line-up to assess the field, as trainers and grooms standing at the horses' heads ask the animals to stretch out like saddle horses. The winner seems to prance with more elan as it takes the victory lap, blue ribbon fluttering from its bridle.

The mood shifts as a pony lead-line class is on next. Riders may be as young as four or five years of age, astride ponies held by parents who walk alongside. Many a horseman who has gone on to capture an Olympic gold medal began his show career in this event, presenting a picture of enjoyment and fledgling ability.

The hunter division focuses on horses, not riders. Those who judge a working hunter class look for an animal which can offer a safe and comfortable ride out fox hunting, plus give evidence of the stamina needed to last over a chase's many miles. These qualities are manifested in a steady, even pace and a bold, but reliable style of taking fences. A refusal, which can create a hazard to members of the hunt field behind such a recalcitrant animal, is deemed a serious fault. Even closer to the spectacle of the sport are appointments and Corinthian classes. The appearance of the horse and rider are taken into consideration in the former, together with their way of going. Complete regalia must be used, right down to a real sandwich in the box fastened to the saddle (at least one competitor finished out of the ribbons when she overlooked that detail, the judge's face turning as green as the moldy matter he extracted). Corinthian, a word meaning amateur sportsman, is open only to members of a hunt. An entry will sometimes be three of them galloping over fences in single file, all resplendent in scarlet coats and hunt caps or top hats.

Saddle horse classes provide equine high fashion. As described in the chapter on the American Saddle Horse, these beauties live for the show ring, primped and preened like debutantes. There is audience participation in the five-gaited class—the crowd's traditional vociferous response to the announcer's instruction to "rack on!", cheering their favorites as the animals speed by.

A Western pleasure event is another change of pace. Instead of flat saddles and somber hacking jackets, the arena is filled with ornate stock saddles and riders in ten-gallon hats and spangled shirts. Like their Eastern equitation counterparts, riders ask their horses to move at the natural gaits, here called walk, jog, and lope. Working under a loose rein, the animals are judged with regard to offering an easy and enjoyable ride.

The last classes of the day may be the presentation of championships in the various divisions. Nothing more is required at this point than for the winners to accept trophies and ribbons emblematic of the highest aggregate scores in several classes within their divisions. As horses are vanned away or bedded down, both winning and losing riders reflect on their performances, resolving to improve for the next show.

The three-day event is a type of competition which requires

Awaiting the call for a hunter seat class. Winning a blue ribbon depends on horse's and rider's preparation, the quality of the competition, and luck, enough uncertainty to make any exhibitor apprehensive.

chosen rodeoing on the professional level as a way of life are a special breed. Unlike most other athletes, they draw no salaries, paying all expenses out of their own pockets. Costs for even a few months are considerable: lodging and stabling, food and feed, gasoline and auto repairs, medical and veterinarian fees. Of course, these sums can be offset by winnings—a top rodeo performer can earn in excess of $50,000 a year plus more from endorsing products—but there must be more of an incentive than just the pot of gold at the end of the "suicide circuit," the way competitors refer to the professional tour. Some say rodeoing is one of the very few ways a man can assert his individuality in this technological, conformist world. To succeed involves pitting his own skills and courage against equine and taurine wiles and power with the knowledge that physical risk is ever-present. Few serious competitors have not been the victim of a mishap, but they keep going back for more.

As on the range, a rodeo cowboy is only as good as his horse, whether his own or the ones he draws for bucking events. Those used in the latter way are as much rugged individuals as the men who try to outlast them. In the early days of the sport, they were obtained from bands of wild mustangs which had never seen, much less been ridden by humans. Excellent bucking horses in the arena, they were terrified by the sound of crowds cheering, which drove them through fences and any other obstacle in their paths. They were just too dangerous for man and other beasts. The alternative was to use horses which were more accustomed to people yet refused to be broken to the saddle. They were not really malicious (although some did have a killer instinct); it was merely a case of an animal's feeling somewhat indignant about having anyone on its back and doing something about dislodging him. Once there was no dearth of buckers, but when rodeo suppliers discovered they were running out of suitable stock, they were forced to raise their own. Stockmen scoured the countryside to find animals with a propensity to buck, and these and their descendents, along with others of all breeds and from all over who are just plumb untamable, are the ones which offer the tough challenge to bronc riders. The horses are not trained to buck. They do it naturally, for no one has taken the time and patience to school them to accept a human burden. There are, however, certain man-made incentives which encourage broncos to perform.

Some people claim that flank straps and cattle prods are cruel, while others defend the practice by saying that the goads merely discomfort, not injure the horses. Moreover, the animals work for a maximum of ten seconds at a time before the straps are loosened, a short time for such strenuous activities. Riders' spurring, too, is more a gesture than actual punishment. Nevertheless, these "outlaw" horses do not feign their movements—ask any rider. The horses' names reflect their idiosyncracies ("Sunfish" and "Bottoms Up") and the consequences of riding them (the celebrated "Widow Maker" and "Ambulance").

Rodeo contestants begin training at an early age, perhaps in high school or younger. Everyone remembers the first time, after having had to hold back tears from jarring falls, he finally lasted eight or ten seconds on a bronc. One doesn't just sign up for a major rodeo and go home with top money; it is a long haul, losing to better men and picking up hints in the process. One way for a performer to increase his skills is to enroll in any of the schools conducted by rodeo stars. The instructors, themselves former or present champions, spend many hours each day sharing their expertise and criticizing pupils' techniques. Videotape helps a rider see what he did wrong and ways to correct any such faults. These seminars have proved so successful that an instructor has often found himself losing out later in the year to a former pupil whom he might have taught "too much." But it takes more than learning to make a rodeo rider into a world's champion. He must have natural ability, a strong desire to win, and the stamina to compete in as many shows as possible to amass the greatest number of points to earn the belt buckle bearing "World's Champion All-Around Cowboy."

The rodeo itself begins with a grand entry. To rousing band music, all the contestants and officials ride around the arena, its illumination reflecting the rainbow colors of clothing, tack, and flags.

Bareback bronc riding may be the first event. Brute strength on the part of the rider is essential to remain astride a pitching four-legged roller coaster with nothing to hold on to but a grip (using one hand at that) fastened to a girth around the horse's belly. He must last for eight seconds, not exactly the twinkling of an eye to anyone concentrating on keeping his balance while spurring the bronc's flanks (if he can locate them). Horses do not just jump up and down

Chariot racing, Old West variety. Any activity involving horses became fair game for rodeo events, the rougher the better.

Hunt clubs sprang up toward the end of the last century in the Northeast, particularly on Long Island and outside of Boston. There are now 112 packs from Massachusetts to California recognized by the Masters of Foxhounds Association. They seek live foxes or conduct drag hunts, where hounds follow a scent laid down several hours before from a sack of animal entrails or droppings.

The hunting season is divided into two parts. Cubbing, during which young hounds are taught their role, takes place from September to November. It is more informal than the regular season lasting until March or April when vixens whelp and Spring's "stinking violets" make scents impossible to follow. Riders following the hounds may wear hacking clothes when out cubbing, but traditional regalia is called for thereafter. Most items of the latter stemmed from practical reasons: a reinforced top hat or bowler offers protection against head injuries in a spill, a stock tie can make an impromptu sling, while the crooked handle of a hunting crop enables a rider to open or close a gate without having to dismount. The black velvet cap and scarlet coat (called "hunting pink" not for the color but after the English tailor who devised the garment) are the exclusive province of the Master and his assistants, shared only with those who have been given the right to wear them. Otherwise, a gentleman member wears a black coat, canary yellow vest, white breeches, and mahogany boots (black with brown tops). Women dress in the same fashion, except they wear solid black boots and always a black coat. Occasionally a woman will ride sidesaddle, in a long black skirt decorously covering her legs. As a rule, personal preference and an individual pack's customs govern choice of appointments. Horses carry English saddles to which may be attached a sandwich box or flask for its rider's refreshment. If there is a martingale, it should be of the standing variety.

A Master of Foxhounds has been likened to a commander-in-chief, and the analogy is not misplaced. It is more than courtesy for all to obey his requests, for he has the authority to send home anyone whom he considers a menace to hounds or the field. Fox hunting is in a sense a spectator sport; not to interfere with the Master is both proper etiquette and the best way to help him and his assistants go about their tasks. The Master is aided by a number of hunt servants, a Huntsman and Whippers-in (shortened to Whips). The Huntsman

Riding sidesaddle harkens back to fox hunting's early days.

controls and signals the hounds, helped by the Whips in keeping them together as a working unit (some Masters act as their own Huntsmen). A Field Master is responsible for the conduct of riders following the pack, setting the pace and distance behind.

Some hunts welcome visitors for a day's sport on payment of a "capping" fee, placed in the Secretary's outstretched headgear. (A member friend can help you secure an invitation or you can contact the Secretary in that regard.) Be sure to arrive well before the designated hour, customarily close to daybreak. You will see members and guests riding up or unloading their horses from vans. With the request " 'ware hounds," hunt servants escort the pack through the crowd. As befitting a guest and a beginner, you keep your voice low and see that your horse avoids coming close to hounds. For the same reasons of manners and experience, do not join the head of the column when the field moves out after the pack—barring mishap, you will not miss anything by being toward the rear.

A likely spot to locate a fox is called a covert. You will have traveled to it at a walk or trot; there is reason to conserve energy for what lies ahead, so an unnecessary gallop or jump is bad form. The Huntsman signals his hounds into the covert. They draw it by sniffing around, urged on by hunt servants' encouraging tones. Perhaps a hound will pick up a scent, speaking tentatively, then louder. Other hounds move over to investigate, their voices joining in. His rest disturbed, the fox should decide to vacate the area. A Whip stationed nearby spots him and gestures to the Huntsman or Master, the latter blowing a "gone away" call on his horn (little more than a mouthpiece which emits piercing toots which can be heard over long distances). Hounds race away in full cry flanked by Whips, while the field readies to join in the chase.

This is the time your horse can show its mettle. His gallop covers the ground easily, yet he is responsive to your hands and legs as you make certain you are a proper length behind the rider in front of you, far enough back to avoid compounding or creating any injury in case he falls or refuses a jump. Your horse pauses to balance before taking a ditch or post-and-rail, then soars over. A fit hunter shows no signs of tiring after many miles, stopping only when the field waits for hounds to recapture the scent. A few moments later someone shouts "Tally-ho!" sighting the fox a meadow away. The chase

227

As an opponent checks to avoid a "crossing over" penalty, a player readies for a forehand smash.

GLOSSARY

action—The movement of a horse's legs, especially with regard to height.

aids—Signals given a horse by a rider, or the methods by which he gives them, such as voice, rein and leg pressure, and spur.

albino—A pure white coat color, very unusual.

bay—A horse with any shade of brown coat and black mane and tail.

barrel—The part of a horse's body around its ribs.

bit—The part of the bridle designed to fit in a horse's mouth.

blacksmith—A person who shoes hooves.

blaze—A white stripe extending the length of a horse's face.

bloodline—A horse's pedigree emphasizing inheritable traits such as speed, endurance, and conformation.

bottom—A term for endurance or stamina.

breed—A group of animals which reproduce the characteristics by which the group is defined.

breeding—The science of mating horses. Selective breeding involves carefully choosing individuals to be mated to obtain features such as conformation, and performance.

bridle—A horse's headgear by which the bit is kept in place.

cannon—That part of the horse's leg between fetlock and hock or knee, corresponding to a human's forearm.

canter—A three-beat gait.

cantle—The rear portion of a saddle.

chest—That part of a horse's body from its forelegs to its neck.

chestnut—A horse with a light brown coat, mane and tail.

chukker—A period of play in polo, lasting seven and one-half minutes.

claiming race—A race in which a horse entered may be purchased before the race for a stipulated price.

collection—A compact and well-balanced position of a standing or moving horse.

colt—A male horse under the age of four.

conformation—A horse's body build, the sum of its individual features.

coronet—That part of a horse's leg between its hoof and fetlock.

covert—An area providing shelter to foxes.

crossbreed—To mate a sire and dam of different breeds. Also, the product of such a mating.

curb—A variety of bit to control head carriage and speed, used alone in Western riding or with a snaffle in English-style to comprise a full bridle.

dam—A horse's mother.

diagonals—A method of posting to the trot, rising relative to either of the horse's forelegs.

dressage—The training or presentation of horse and rider through natural, collected and extended gaits and figures, stressing responsiveness and balance.

driver—The man who guides a harness horse in a trotting or pacing race.

equitation—A horse show class in which only the rider's performance is judged. Also, horsemanship in general.

extension—A position of a standing or moving horse in which its stride is longer than is naturally done, the opposite of collection.

farrier—A blacksmith.

fetlock—That part of the horse's leg between the pastern and the cannon, bearing a tuft of hair.

field—The riders who follow a fox hunting pack. Also, racehorses grouped together as a betting unit.

filly—A female horse under four years of age.

forequarters—The part of a horse up to its barrel.

forge—(of a horse)—To strike a foreleg with a hind leg while trotting.

forward seat—A style of equitation in which the rider keeps his weight over the horse's forequarters, used for jumping.

frog—The soft underpart of a hoof.

gait—Any of a horse's movements distinguished by leg patterns; gaits consist of walk, trot, canter, gallop, pace, slow gait, and rack.

gallop—A similar (but faster) gait to the canter. A hand gallop is slower than a true gallop or run.

gaskin—That portion of a horse's hind leg between the hock and stifle.

gelding—A male horse which has been castrated.

get—The offspring of a stallion. A stallion "stamps his get" when his children resemble him in certain traits.

girth—A strap to hold a saddle or harness in place, fastened under a horse's belly.

green—A horse whose training has not been completed.

grey—A horse whose coat is a mixture of black and white hairs.

hand—The unit of measurement for horses, equal to four inches; height is measured from the ground to the withers. "In hand" means exhibited without saddle.

handicap—A race in which each horse carries an amount of weight based on its ability in an attempt to equalize chances of winning. Also, to try to predict a race's outcome by analyzing entrants' chances.

harness—Leather apparatus by which a horse is attached to a vehicle which it will pull.

hind quarters—The part of a horse behind its barrel.

hock—That joint of a horse's leg between cannon and gaskin corresponding to a human's elbow.

hunter—A horse used for fox hunting, or a suitable type.

hurdle—A jumping race over brush obstacles, or such an obstacle.

jockey—A race horse's rider.

knee—That joint on a horse's foreleg between forearm and cannon, corresponding to a human's elbow.

lead—The first hoof to strike the ground in a canter.

lope—A Western term for canter.

mare—A female horse four years or older.

martingale—A piece of tack for holding a horse's head down. A standing martingale is a single strap from girth to bridle; a running martingale extends from girth to reins.

near—The left side of a horse.

neck rein—To control a horse's direction by rein pressure on its neck, as opposed to pressure on the bit.

off—The right side of a horse.

pace—A gait in which the horse's lateral legs (on the same side) strike the ground simultaneously.

pastern—That part of the horse's leg between the coronet and fetlock.

pelham—A variety of bit combining curb and snaffle.

poll—The part of a horse's body where its head joins its neck.

pommel—The front of a saddle. Also, the horn on a Western saddle.

pony—Any of certain breeds tending to stand under 14½ hands. Also, any horse used in polo.

post—To rise and fall in the saddle at the trot. Also, the starting point of a race.

prepotent—A stallion's genetic ability to pass specific characteristics to its get.

rack—An artificial gait in which a horse's hooves strike laterally but not quite simultaneously.

remuda—A string of Western horses from which cowboys select their mounts for the day.

school—To train a horse.

shoulder—That part of a horse's body where the foreleg joins the body.

sire—A horse's father.

slow gait—An artificial gait in which a horse's hooves strike the ground in a four-beat, slightly syncopated pattern, also known as the singlefoot.

snaffle—A variety of bit to control direction.

stallion—A male horse four years or older.

steeplechase—A jumping race over wood fences, or jumping races in general.

stifle—The joint of a horse's hind leg which joins the leg to the body.

stockings—White markings on a horse's lower legs.

stretch—The straight portion of a race track. The back stretch is further away from the grandstand, while the home stretch leads to the finish line.

sulky—The light two-wheeled cart drawn by harness racing horses.

tack—Equipment worn by a horse. As a verb, to put the equipment on a horse.

trot—A gait in which the horse's diagonal legs strike the ground simultaneously.

withers—The highest point on a horse where its neck joins its shoulder.